Superstar Cars

Porsche

Robert Walker

CRABTREE
Publishing Company
www.crabtreebooks.com

Author: Robert Walker
Publishing plan research and development:
    Sean Charlebois, Reagan Miller
    Crabtree Publishing Company
Editor: Sonya Newland
Proofreader: Molly Aloian
Editorial director: Kathy Middleton
Project coordinator and prepress technician: Margaret Salter
Print coordinator: Katherine Berti
Series consultant: Petrina Gentile
Cover design: Ken Wright
Design: Bally design
Photo research: Amy Sparks

Photographs:
Alamy: imagebroker: p. 7; Phil Talbot: p. 10, 14 (top), 16–17, 41; vario images GmbH & Co.KG: pp. 1, 48; culture-images GmbH: pp. 13, 29 (top), 34 (top); marassphotography.com: p. 25 (top); Rhea Eason: pp. 26–27; pbpgalleries: pp. 27 (top), 42–43, 45; Mike Oxlade: p. 44, 46
Corbis: Bettmann: p. 6, 20
Dreamstime: Ken Hurst: p. 32 (bottom)
Motoring Picture Library: p. 8, 11, 14–15, 17 (top), 18–19, 21, 22, 23, 24–25, 28–29, 30, 32–33, 34–35, 36–37, 50 (top)
Porsche: p. 1, 4, 31, 43 (top), 49, 50–51, 52–53, 53 (top), 54, 55, 57 (top), 57 (bottom), 58, 59
Shutterstock: front cover; BartlomiejMagierowski: p. 5; Ben Smith: p. 9; Max Earey: pp. 38–39, 39 (top); Algecireño: p. 47

Library and Archives Canada Cataloguing in Publication

Walker, Robert, 1980-
    Porsche / Robert Walker.

(Superstar cars)
Includes index.
Issued also in an electronic format.
ISBN 978-0-7787-2146-8 (bound).--ISBN 978-0-7787-2153-6 (pbk.)

    1. Porsche automobiles--Juvenile literature.
I. Title. II. Series: Superstar cars

TL215.P75W34 2011   j629.222'2   C2010-905634-5

Library of Congress Cataloging-in-Publication Data

Walker, Robert, 1980-
 Porsche / Robert Walker.
    p. cm. -- (Superstar cars)
 Includes index.
 ISBN 978-0-7787-2153-6 (pbk. : alk. paper) --
 ISBN 978-0-7787-2146-8 (reinforced library binding : alk. paper) --
 ISBN 978-1-4271-9551-7 (electronic (pdf))
 1. Porsche automobiles--Juvenile literature. I. Title. II. Series.

 TL215.P75W35 2010
 629.222'2--dc22
                                                        2010034937

Crabtree Publishing Company

www.crabtreebooks.com   1-800-387-7650

Printed in the U.S.A./102010/SP20100915

Published in Canada
Crabtree Publishing
616 Welland Ave.
St. Catharines, ON
L2M 5V6

Published in the United States
Crabtree Publishing
PMB 59051
350 Fifth Avenue, 59th Floor
New York, New York 10118

Published in the United Kingdom
Crabtree Publishing
Maritime House
Basin Road North, Hove
BN41 1WR

Published in Australia
Crabtree Publishing
386 Mt. Alexander Rd.
Ascot Vale (Melbourne)
VIC 3032

>> Contents

Chapter 1

Sleek and Fast

"I couldn't find the sports car of my dreams, so I built it myself." These words were spoken by Ferdinand Anton Ernst "Ferry" Porsche, the driving force behind one of the most popular sports cars of all time. It is this dedication to originality and quality that has guided the Porsche company since it began almost 60 years ago.

A thing of beauty

Speed, power, curves, and style—all of these things come to mind when people think of a Porsche sports car. From the engine and body right down to the gauges on the dashboard, everything on a Porsche car is uniquely Porsche. Each part comes together to create a vehicle that is the desire of driving enthusiasts everywhere.

The making of a legend

Since the first Porsche sports car was built in 1948, the company has set out to surpass its achievements with each new series and model. Series like the 356 and the 911 have made the name Porsche synonymous with the highest level of excellence, for cars both on the road and on the racetrack.

Industry leader

In an industry dominated by giants like Mercedes-Benz and Ferrari, Porsche has not only found its own place among sports-car manufacturers, it has also bested the competition many, many times. Innovations such as Porsche's extremely powerful air-cooled rear-mounted engine have set the pace in an industry known for going fast.

Today, the Porsche line of cars is extensive enough to meet the wants and needs of almost any motorist.

A Porsche sports car such as the Boxster is instantly recognizable by its style and design—not to mention its speed!

Dr. Ferdinand Anton Porsche, Sr.

Born in 1875, the founder of the Porsche company, Ferdinand Porsche Sr., was always fascinated with anything mechanical. At the age of 25, he helped design and build the Lohner-Porsche electric car, which was displayed at the Paris World's Fair. Dr. Porsche also helped construct a car that ran on a combination of gasoline and electricity. This **hybrid car** was almost 100 years ahead of its time.

The name behind the car

The Porsche company was founded in 1931 by Dr. Ferdinand Porsche Sr. in Stuttgart, Germany. With a résumé that included previous work for Mercedes-Benz and other automakers, Ferdinand was soon commissioned by the German government to build a practical, affordable car for the German people. He set about designing the Volkswagen, which developed into the now very familiar Volkswagen Beetle.

Automotive skills

By the end of 1935, Ferdinand Sr. and company had three **prototypes** up and running, and in 1939 the first Volkswagen was displayed at the

Dr. Ferdinand Porsche Sr. founder of the Porsche company, gives a demonstration to his workers in Germany in the 1940s.

Berlin Automobile Show. The Porsche company also designed and built a racing **coupe** called the Type 60K10. This **speedster** was supposed to take part in a Berlin-to-Rome race to showcase Germany's automotive skills to the rest of the world. Plans for the race were abandoned, however, as Nazi Germany turned all of its efforts toward World War II.

A family affair

When Ferdinand Sr. began his auto-motive design business in 1939, several members of the Porsche family were involved with the company. One of Porsche's first employees was a young Ferry Porsche, Ferdinand's son. It would be Ferry Porsche who later designed the 356 model, a car whose popularity helped Porsche become a leader in the sports-car industry.

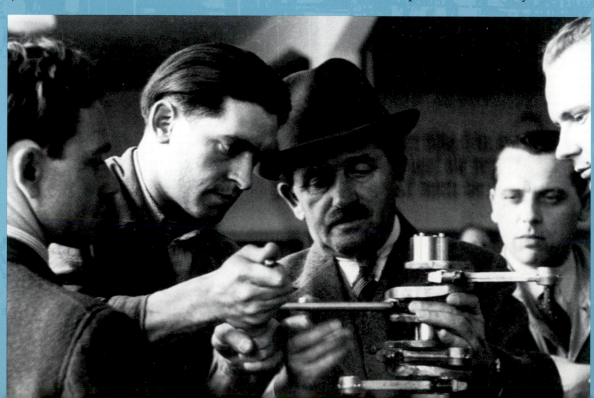

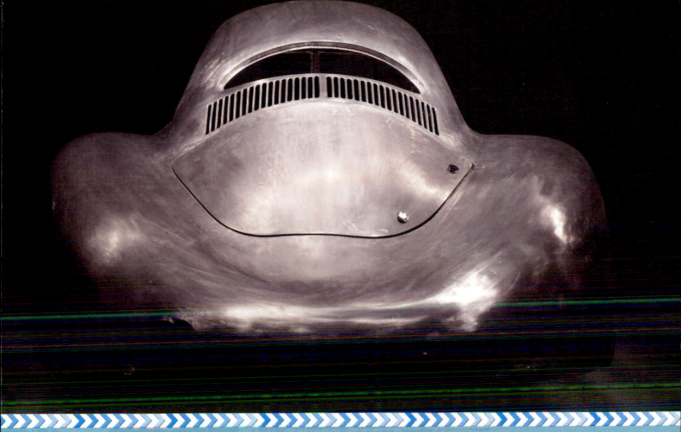

 Only one example of the Porsche Type 60K10 is known to exist today. This strange-looking speedster sat low to the ground and had doors that opened diagonally upward.

The next generation

Porsche would remain a family-run company for almost 30 years, until the Porsche family stepped down as managers in the early 1970s. But Porsche family members would be responsible for many of Porsche's successes over the years. Ferdinand Sr.'s grandson, Ferdinand Alexander "Butzi" Porsche, served as head of design for over ten years, and helped create the 911—one of Porsche's most popular and enduring vehicles.

Vital Statistics

Type 60K10

Production years: 1939
No. built: 3
Top speed: 99 mph (160 km/h)
Engine type: Flat-four, air-cooled
Engine size: 1.5 liters, 50 hp
Cylinders: 4
Transmission: Manual
CO_2 emissions: N/A
EPA fuel economy ratings: N/A
Price: N/A

‣‣ Humble beginnings

The Porsche automotive design company started in the family garage. Simple surroundings would continue for the small business until wartime bombing forced Ferdinand Sr. to move Porsche operations out of Stuttgart and into a converted sawmill in Gmund, Austria, in 1944.

Even with the company's modest appearance, however, it wasn't long before demand enabled Porsche to grow. Along with his work for the German government, Ferdinand Sr. was also commissioned by the Auto Union Company to help design a new racing car for the Grand Prix circuit.

Designer for the Nazis

Earning the title "Automotive Designer for the Reich" (the Reich was the German state), Ferdinand Sr. was ordered by the Nazi government to design tanks and other vehicles that could be used in the war effort. His design work included the Leopard Tiger tank and the Maus tank. This work put Ferdinand Sr.'s plans for car development almost completely on hold.

■ Ferdinand Porsche with his Auto Union racecar. It was this project that began the mid-to-rear engine placement for which Porsche became famous.

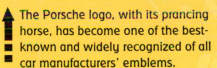 The Porsche logo, with its prancing horse, has become one of the best-known and widely recognized of all car manufacturers' emblems.

Porsche interrupted

When Germany was defeated in the war, Porsche's military service came to an end. Unfortunately for Ferdinand Sr., at the end of World War II he was jailed by the French for his work for the Nazis. He spent two years in a French prison. During this time, Ferry and his sister Louise took the reins of Porsche and began work on the projects that would shape the company for the next 20 years.

The Porsche logo

The Porsche emblem was finalized in 1952. It looks a lot like the Ferrari logo, with its black horse on a yellow shield. This image is the coat-of-arms of Stuttgart, Germany, where Porsche's main base of operations is located. The city of Stuttgart takes its name from the German word for horse stud farm, "Stuotgarten." The background of the Porsche logo is the crest of the State of Baden-Württemberg, Germany.

Chapter 2

>> The Car That Made the Company

When Ferdinand Sr. returned to the company, work was already underway on what would become the 356. Led by Ferdinand's son, Ferry, the Porsche team struggled to design and construct the car in postwar Germany. This wasn't easy, as parts and other resources were hard to come by in a country exhausted by a long and costly war.

The 356/1

By 1948, the first working prototype of the 356, the 356/1, was up and running. With a tubular frame, open top, and a 1131 cc air-cooled engine, the 356/1 borrowed heavily from the Volkswagen, including the engine and other parts. Wanting to test the car's abilities, Ferry's cousin, Herbert, drove the 356/1 in a race at the Innsbruck Stadtrennen—and won. This was less than a month after the car was completed!

The 356/2

The 356/2 was a two-door coupe with the Volkswagen engine moved to the rear. This placement made the car easier to construct and left more luggage space. The 356/2 was unveiled at the Geneva Auto Show in 1949, to mostly positive reviews. Encouraged by the public response, Porsche began producing its **flagship** vehicle—52 cars in all.

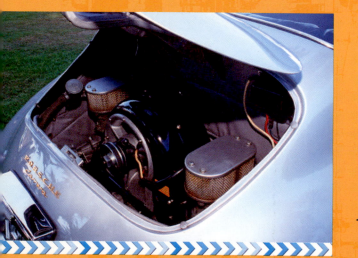

Taking the reins

After his release from prison, the aging Ferdinand Porsche Sr. was in very poor health. It fell to Ferry Porsche and others to take over control of the company. Ferdinand Sr.'s health worsened, and he passed away in 1951.

◄ ■■

Beginning with the 356/2, the air-cooled engine was placed in the rear of the car.

Like the cabriolet version, the 356 Pre-A 1100 coupe featured a split windshield, which was separated by a support bar.

The finished product

The Porsche company returned to Stuttgart and started churning out the 356 series at a rate of 33 cars a month. By the end of 1950, almost 300 Porsches had been sold. The Pre-A series included the 1100 coupe version and the 1100 cabriolet. The Volkswagen engine of both cars was increased to 1286 cc, with 44 **horsepower** (hp). **Hydraulic** brakes and a fully synchronized **transmission** were also added.

Vital Statistics

356 Pre-A 1100 Coupe

Production years: 1950–54
No. built: 6,252 (includes all engine versions)
Top speed: 87 mph (140 km/h)
Engine type: Flat-four, air-cooled, rear-placement
Engine size: 1086 cc (1.1 liter), 40 bhp
Cylinders: 4
Transmission: 4-speed manual
CO_2 emissions: N/A
EPA fuel economy ratings: 40 mpg
Price: 11,400 Deutschmarks (approx. US$2,700) (1954)

Base of operations

The new Stuttgart facility started as a small combination of offices and a design area. When it first opened, the shop was just big enough inside for two cars and a team of four mechanics.

As interest in Porsche grew, so did its facilities in Germany. Over time, more designers and assembly workers were added to its roster to keep up with demand, and the facility expanded.

■ The huge production facility at Stuttgart, Germany, is split by a large public road. Porsche built a bridge over it to connect its body shop and paint shop.

Testing grounds

It is in Weissach, Germany, that all of Porsche's research and development takes place. Considered by many to be the cradle of Porsche, Weissach has been the birthplace of every Porsche car since 1974. Weissach is also the heart of racecar development and production. In 2006, the new Porsche motorsport center was completed. It is here that Porsche focuses on continuing its tradition of excellence in racing.

AMAZING FACTS

Uphill climb

The first road tests of the 356 prototype were done on the Katschberg Pass in Austria. The new car was made to climb up the steep mountain route, in a series of performance tests, to an elevation of 5,384 feet (1,641 m). Today, Porsche continues to conduct its uphill tests on mountain roads.

 There is as much road at the Porsche testing grounds as there is in some small towns! The company is known for its exhaustive testing in the process of developing its vehicles.

Porsche production

The main Porsche plant and offices are located in Stuttgart-Zuffenhausen, Germany, with several large buildings along the sprawling property. Today, almost all Porsche engines are made in Stuttgart-Zuffenhausen. Production has grown to include factories in Ludwigsburg, Leipzig, and Weissach, Germany. They employ thousands of men and women.

Planning for the future

Porsche has a reputation for always looking ahead. It dedicates more time, money, and manpower to the processes of research and development than almost any other automotive manufacturer.

Almost 20 percent of Porsche employees work at the testing grounds at Weissach. Facilities there include a **state-of-the-art** wind tunnel, design departments, and miles of private road for test-driving vehicles.

≫ A star is born

In 1956, Porsche launched the next car in its 356 series, the 356A. The A cars were noticeably more comfortable than earlier Porsches, with improved handling and a new engine that offered 60 hp at 4,500 rpm. The support bar was also removed from the windshield. This marked the first of several versions of the 356 that Porsche released over its almost 15-year run.

One of the distinguishing features of the 356C 1600 is the use of two separate grilles on the rear engine cover. Many Porsche enthusiasts refer to this model as the "twin grille."

Vital Statistics

**365A 1600
Super Coupe**

Production years: 1956–59
No. built: 13,016 (all engine versions)
Top speed: 108.5 mph (175 km/h)
Engine type: Flat-four, air-cooled, rear-placement
Engine size: 1582 cc (1.6 liter), 75 bhp
Cylinders: 4
Transmission: 4-speed manual
CO_2 emissions: N/A
EPA fuel economy ratings: 34 mpg
Price: 13,800 Deutschmarks (approx. US$3,300) (1958)

356 variations

The 356 series included the release of the 356A 1600 Super, 356A 1600 Convertible D, 356C 1600, and the 356 Carrera 2000 GS. Each model was made to be an improvement on its predecessor, offering more speed, style, and comfort than the one before. The Carrera 2000 GS was particularly notable for its extremely powerful engine at the time, which could reach speeds of over 124 mph (200 km/h). Today the 2000 GS is much sought after by collectors, as few were produced.

Under the hood

Porsche 356 engines were noticeably different from other sports-car engines of the time. The rear-mounted, air-cooled, four-cylinder boxer engine became a defining feature of Porsche cars. Also, there was no oil pan; instead the oil was held in the crankcase and taken by a pump to the moving parts of the engine, before being cooled and sent through again. Also, Porsche engines had developed a reputation for being very, very loud!

In its 15-year production run, the 356 series engine underwent many changes and improvements. Porsche offered several engine versions per model.

PORSCHE
RC·7752
NY EMPIRE STATE 60

≫ A deal with Volkswagen

Porsche and Volkswagen have a long history of working together. Both companies had something the other wanted. Porsche had the design expertise and ingenuity, Volkswagen had the parts. A formal agreement in 1948 allowed Porsche use of Volks-wagen materials, as well as their sales resources. In return, Porsche would help Volkswagen in the development and testing of its own automobiles.

The 914 collaboration

For the next two decades, Porsche played a major role in almost 60 Volkswagen car projects. One of their most famous collaborations was a joint project in the late 1960s to create a new sports car called the 914. Two versions of the 914 were built—a four-cylinder that was released by Volkswagen, and a considerably sportier six-cylinder released by Porsche.

Not a "glorified Beetle"

The 356 series did have many similarities with the Volkswagen that Ferdinand Sr. helped design before the end of World War II. From its earliest years and throughout the 1960s, the 356 shared many parts with the Volkswagen. These included the engine, cable-operated brakes, gearbox, and rear-swing axle.

The similarities under the hood led some doubters to dismiss Porsche cars as nothing more than **souped-up** Volkswagens. While it's true the early Porsche engines were Volkswagen, they were still engines that had been designed by Porsche. Also, the modified 40 hp Volkswagen engines underwent many changes in order to provide the power and speed expected in a sports car.

 While the early Porsches borrowed heavily from the moving parts of a Volkswagen, the 356 series had a look and style all its own.

 The 914 was a collaboration between Porsche and Volkswagen in the 1960s. The resulting Porsche sports car was known for its speed and handling.

⟩⟩ Growing pains

Even with its tremendous early success with the 356 series, Porsche had to overcome a number of difficulties in getting the car off the ground. There were design issues, such as the early unsynchronized gearbox, which could lead to very unpleasant grinding. But perhaps the biggest problem was finding a permanent home that allowed Porsche to meet the growing demand for the 356.

Finding a home

The wartime Porsche facility in Gmund just wasn't enough in terms of space or resources if the company was going to succeed. Plans to return to the original factory in Stuttgart were brought to a standstill because the United States military had taken up residence there. A date was set for the return of the factory to the Porsche company, but the delay greatly interfered with production. Porsche was forced to open up a new workshop in Stuttgart, only a short distance from the old works.

Facing the competition

When the 356 came on the scene, its unusual appearance made it stand out from most other sports cars of the time. Some found the shape squat, and less than appealing. The 356 design was admittedly shorter than some other sports cars, such as the long and sleek Jaguar XK 120. But many car magazines and sport enthusiasts praised the 356's curves and refreshing, attention-grabbing design.

Peak performance

The 356 engine may not have been as powerful as some other sports-car manufacturers' engines, but its performance struck a chord with drivers. As sales increased overseas, Porsche began gearing up to break into North America. The U.S. automotive market was dominated by larger, American-made cars like Ford and GM. It wouldn't be easy for Porsche to impress a public that was still relatively new to the idea of a sports car for everyday use.

Although the basic look and design of the 356 series remained the same, improvements were made with each model. This is the 356B 1600.

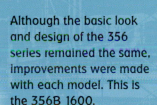

Vital Statistics

356B 1600 Super 90 Roadster

Production years: 1960–62
No. built: 2,902 (all engine versions)
Top speed: 112 mph (180 km/h)
Engine type: Flat-four, air-cooled, rear-placement
Engine size: 1582 cc (1.6 liter), 90 bhp
Cylinders: 4
Transmission: 4-speed manual
CO_2 emissions: N/A
EPA fuel economy ratings: 32.6 mpg
Price: 15,200 Deutschmarks (approx. US$3,645) (1960)

Chapter 3

≫Porsche in America ≫≫≫≫≫≫

Before 1950, sports cars were something of a rarity on American roadways. Most people only saw them on the racetrack or with their favorite celebrity behind the wheel. The average driver relied instead on automotive giants such as Ford or General Motors for their vehicles. Some sports-car makers such as Jaguar and Mercedes-Benz had been able to break into the American auto market, but it was still a relatively small niche.

Across the sea

Porsche understood the nature of the American auto economy it was entering. The young company realized the important role the United States would play in its future. Luckily for Porsche, the postwar automotive market in the United States was changing. Interest was beginning to grow in sports cars. By adapting to the demands of the American driver, Porsche had a real shot at finding success in the United States.

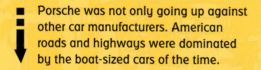
Porsche was not only going up against other car manufacturers. American roads and highways were dominated by the boat-sized cars of the time.

A change in the market

With the onset of World War II, much of the American automotive industry joined the rest of the country in the war effort. The priority had switched from making cars to providing the military with the machines they needed to fight overseas. Most car production was put on hold for the war's duration, which made for a shortage of new cars in North America when the war ended. After the war, most automakers picked up where they left off in terms of designs, producing cars that closely resembled models from almost five years previous. A lot of disappointed customers wished for something different, something new.

The racing circuit

Stock car racing was also growing in popularity, with an increasing number of people flocking to the track. More and more drivers were looking for lighter, faster cars to satisfy their "need for speed." These changes were just the sort of thing sports car manufacturers such as Porsche and Ferrari were hoping for—people who wanted newer, different, and faster cars.

Stock car racing was on the rise in the United States, and drivers were looking for lighter and faster cars—like this sporty 356B—that would help them win.

...itting in

With the arrival of the first 356 cars in the United States, it didn't take long to see that some changes were needed to succeed in this new market. One such change came with the introduction of the Type 527 1500 cc engine. Changes were also made to the instrumentation and braking systems. The spare tire in the front storage area was repositioned to allow for more baggage space.

Heavyweight 356

One interesting aspect of the 356 remained, however—it's heavy rear end. With so much weight on the back, the 356 could swing out dangerously when taking a curve too quickly. But this characteristic became something of a bond among Porsche drivers, as all rear-engined cars required a breaking-in period. They still do today.

■ A poster advertising the 356 in 1955.
■ Some modifications were made to meet the demands of the new American market.

The world's most talked-about car

PORSCHE
Typ 356

Max Hoffman

A racecar driver in his youth, Max Hoffman moved to the United States in 1947 and founded the Hoffman Motor Company. He worked with big-name foreign carmakers such as Fiat, Jaguar, and Mercedes-Benz to bring their cars to the United States. He is credited with helping guide the design of the popular Mercedez-Benz 300SL sports car.

PORSCHE
473 FM

Dealer's choice

Much of Porsche's early success in the United States can be attributed to one man—Max Hoffman. An Austrian, Hoffman worked as an **importer** of foreign cars to America, including BMW and Alfa Romeo. Hoffman saw the need for a lighter, more affordable 356 in America. It should have all the speed of a racer but still be able to drive home from the track…

So was born the Porsche Speedster in 1955, which offered drivers the power of a Porsche at a lower cost (under US$3,000). The first Speedsters were trimmed-down versions of the Pre-A 356 series, with removable side curtains in place of rollup windows. Also, to cut down on weight, the interiors were very minimal, with no glove box and very simple instrumentation.

■ Some people thought the Porsche Speedster looked like an upside-down bathtub!

Vital Statistics

356 1500 Speedster

Production years: 1955
No. built: 1,234 (all engine versions)
Top speed: 99 mph (160 km/h)
Engine type: Flat-four, air-cooled, rear-placement
Engine size: 1488 cc (1.5 liter), 55 bhp
Cylinders: 4
Transmission: 4-speed manual
CO_2 emissions: N/A
EPA fuel economy ratings: 38 mpg
Price: 12,200 Deutschmarks (approx. US$2,900) (1954)

Made for America

From the beginning, Porsche intended to make cars for sale only in the United States. These models would be geared toward American drivers—although later on, they would be offered to European motorists as well. Another example, the American **Roadster**, was also Hoffman-inspired. This lightweight, aluminum-bodied racer came with a 1488 cc pushrod engine and could be easily stripped of any superfluous weight. While popular with some racers at the time, it failed to garner enough interest and the Roadster was soon discontinued.

Successful speedsters

But other Americanized 356s would find a place in the United States. The Convertible D in 1959 was the successor to the popular Speedster and also proved successful. It sold over 1,300 units during its production run. The 356B also found an audience when it was introduced in 1960. Porsche continued the Americanization of its cars to include all future models— and continues to do so today.

Looking forward

By the mid-1960s, the 356 series was coming to its end. For almost 15 years the popularity of the 356 had helped Porsche become an industry leader in sports cars. Sales of the 356 had risen to almost 10,000 each year. This was quite an accomplishment, especially since initial projections in 1949 were that the 356 would sell around 500—in total!

With faster, more powerful engines and sleeker lines, every inch of the car was constantly reviewed and improved upon. It was this dedication to change that led Porsche to the decision to release its next series—the 911. This revolutionary design would take Porsche into the next century.

The Americanized version of the 356 series—including the 356C, pictured here—continued to grow steadily in popularity throughout its production run.

American Roadster

Production years: 1952–53
No. built: 21
Top speed: 112 mph (180 km/h)
Engine type: Flat-four, air-cooled,
  rear-placement pushrod
Engine size: 1488 cc (1.5 liter),
  70 bhp
Cylinders: 4
Transmission: 4-speed manual
CO2 emissions: N/A
EPA fuel economy ratings: 37 mpg
  (city); 76–100 mpg (highway)
Price: US$4,600 (1953)

Always with an eye on the horizon,
Porsche made subtle changes in the
356 each year it was in production.

►► Porsche on track

Porsche has a distinguished history in the world of professional motor sports. Even in its early years, the young company dedicated much of its efforts to succeeding on the track. From 1954 to 1956 alone, Porsche took home over 400 racing victories from competitions around the world.

The "Giant Killer"

After finishing work on what would be his last movie, "Giant," actor James Dean hopped behind the wheel of his 550 Spyder and sped off to a semiprofessional race. En route he collided with another car. Dean died shortly after, and since then the 550 Spyder has been associated with the loss of the film star.

Along came a Spyder

Much of Porsche's early success on the racetrack is owed to the 550 Spyder. Put into production in 1954, this was initially known as just the 550, but importer Max Hoffman convinced Porsche that American motorists prefer names for their cars instead of just numbers.

The 550 Spyder came with a light aluminum body and featured a fast four-cam mid-engine. With a top speed of almost 150 mph (241 km/h), the 550 Spyder could outrace other cars of its time that were bigger and more powerful. The Spyder was considered by many to be the top small-displacement racer in the whole world.

The 550 Spyder was relatively expensive for the time, costing almost US$7,000 (about US$56,000 today). ▪▪➡

Carrera Panamericana

Begun in 1950 to celebrate the opening of the Pan-American highway, the Carrera Panamericana road race was considered by many at the time to be the most difficult in the world. In 1953 and 1954, Porsche 550 Spyders won in their class. In honor of this world-famous race, Porsche would use the name for some of its cars in later years.

The 1962 Porsche 804 Grand Prix car. This was the year that the company won its first Grand Prix race.

The Targa Florio

The Targa Florio was an incredibly challenging endurance race that ran through the mountains of Sicily. Porsche took home its first victory there in 1956 with the 550 A Spyder. The automaker would go on to win the Targa Florio ten more times by 1973. Porsche would also use the name of this race for some of its future models.

Vital Statistics

The 550 Spyder

Production years: 1954–56
No. built: 90
Top speed: 136 mph (220 km/h)
Engine type: Four-cam, air-cooled, rear-placement
Engine size: 1498 cc (1.5 liter), 110 bhp
Cylinders: 4
Transmission: 4-speed manual
CO_2 emissions: N/A
EPA fuel economy ratings: 30 mpg
Price: 24,600 Deutschmarks (US$5,900) (1956)

Chapter 4

≫ A New Era for Porsche ≫≫≫≫

The 1960s marked a time of great change for Porsche. Production of the 356 had come to an end, and the company was preparing to unveil what it hoped to be the next big thing in sports cars—the 911. Unveiled to the world at the 1963 Frankfurt Auto Show in Germany, the 911 was a completely new look for Porsche. More space, more glass, a bigger and more powerful engine—the 911 signaled a new direction for the company.

Taking a chance

By replacing its number-one car with the new 911, Porsche was taking a pretty big risk. A large amount of company money and effort had gone into designing and building the 911, and its failure could mean serious financial trouble. Not only that, but Porsche risked alienating loyal customers and car enthusiasts alike by replacing the popular 356 with another model.

Changing tastes

Drivers' tastes were changing. They wanted more luggage space, bigger seats, a powerful but quieter engine—and sports-car manufacturers were responding in kind. Porsche's plans for a new car had been in the making as far back as 1956. The 356's replacement was designed to resemble its predecessor—thus Porsche paid respect to its past and to its customers' loyalty, while responding to changed circumstances and a new market.

■■➤

Since production began on the 911 in 1965, the car has undergone steady modification without compromising the classic style and refinement of the early models.

Vital Statistics

911 Coupe

Production years: 1965–67
No. built: 6,607
Top speed: 130 mph (210 km/h)
Engine type: Flat-six, air-cooled,
  rear-placement
Engine size: 1991 cc (2 liter), 130 bhp
Cylinders: 6
Transmission: 5-speed manual
CO_2 emissions: N/A
EPA fuel economy ratings: 29.5 mpg
Price: 20,980 Deutschmarks
  (approx. US$5,245) (1966)

! Designing the new 911 cost a lot of money. As a result, Porsche didn't have the funding needed to compete in Formula 1 racing in 1963.

Butzi's big plans

Leading the design of the new car was Ferry Porsche's son, Butzi. Other sportster companies such as Mercedes-Benz and Jaguar were unveiling new and exciting models. Butzi knew that Porsche couldn't just rely on the past if it was going to compete. The 911 should celebrate the past, but it should also show the world the new direction that Porsche would be taking.

›› Meet the 911

The design of the 911 proved difficult for Porsche. Butzi and some of the other designers disagreed on the style, and rising costs of prototypes caused concern. The deadline for the 911's debut at the 1963 Frankfurt Auto Show was fast approaching, and everyone was working very hard to have the car ready on time.

Success!

All the effort paid off in the end. The 911 wowed visitors to the show with its impressive six-cylinder boxer engine, with 130 hp at 6100 rpm, and with a top speed of 131.25 mph (210 km/h). The US$6,500 price tag—lower than that of many a competitor—was also a hit with customers. It would be another full year before the 911 was available to the public, and orders began piling up.

AMAZING FACTS

What's in a name?

Until its debut at the Frankfurt Auto Show in 1963, the Porsche 911 was called the 901. Porsche discovered that the carmaker Peugeot already owned the rights to numbers with a zero in the middle, so Porsche changed the designation to the 911.

The 911S variant had an increased horsepower of 160 and improved suspension, steering, and braking.

More on the way

The public response to the 911 led Porsche to release several models in quick succession. The 1967 911 Targa (named after the famous Targa Florio race) was the first version with an open top. Porsche also released the 912, a more affordable 911, thanks to its use of the engine from the 356 and its stripped-down interior.

Racing victories

Like the 356, the 911 earned victories on the racetrack very early on. It placed seventh in the Monte Carlo Rally in 1965, less than a year after production began. This would be the first of many racing accomplishments for the 911.

The 917 became one of the best-loved sports cars of all time, made famous by its Le Mans wins in 1970 and 1971 and by its starring role in the film *Le Mans*.

Leading car

The Porsche 917 racecar was pretty much the star in the 1971 film "Le Mans." Named after the 24-hour endurance race it focused on, this model was driven by actor Steve McQueen. The movie is famous for having more racing than it does dialogue—no one says a word for almost the first half-hour!

⟫ Changing the formula

As the years passed, Porsche began to move farther away from the designs for which it had become famous. Porsche had always been known for its air-cooled rear-placement engines and distinctive bodies. But for better or worse, by the close of the 1960s this all began to change.

A mid-engine car

In 1969, Porsche's collaboration with Volkswagen on the 914 made for a compact, lighter, and more affordable Porsche. They decided to move the engine closer to the middle of the car, which was a change of pace for Porsche. The 914/4 offered a four-cylinder air-cooled engine with a top speed of 109 mph (174 km/h), at a price of US$3,695.

The 914/6 had a more powerful six-cylinder engine and cost US$6,099, but it was nowhere near as popular as the 914/4. Porsche stopped making the 914/6 after only three years. In its seven-year production run, almost 119,000 of the 914 series were made. This number was considerably lower than Porsche had hoped.

 The 914 remained Porsche's only mid-engine car until the debut of the Boxster several years later.

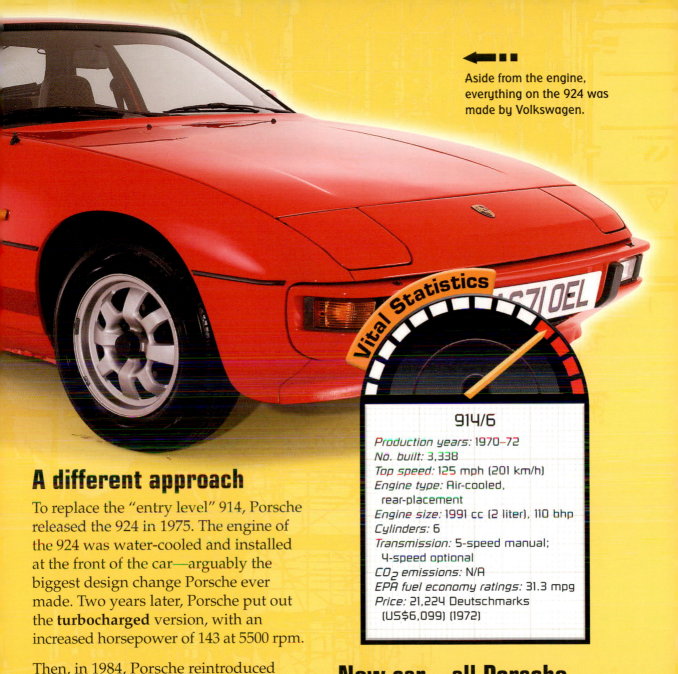

Aside from the engine, everything on the 924 was made by Volkswagen.

Vital Statistics

914/6

Production years: 1970–72
No. built: 3,338
Top speed: 125 mph (201 km/h)
Engine type: Air-cooled,
  rear-placement
Engine size: 1991 cc (2 liter), 110 bhp
Cylinders: 6
Transmission: 5-speed manual;
  4-speed optional
CO_2 emissions: N/A
EPA fuel economy ratings: 31.3 mpg
Price: 21,224 Deutschmarks
  (US$6,099) (1972)

A different approach

To replace the "entry level" 914, Porsche released the 924 in 1975. The engine of the 924 was water-cooled and installed at the front of the car—arguably the biggest design change Porsche ever made. Two years later, Porsche put out the **turbocharged** version, with an increased horsepower of 143 at 5500 rpm.

Then, in 1984, Porsche reintroduced the car as the 924S; it had the same body but with a top speed of 134 mph (216 km/h). Others in the series would follow, but the 924 was never able to achieve the success and popularity of its predecessors. Many Porsche purists criticized the huge part Volkswagen played in the 924's construction. The line was abandoned permanently in 1988.

New car—all Porsche

By the 1970s, Porsche was looking for a car to be the successor to the 911. The company wanted a vehicle that would appeal to a wider audience than just the two-seater speedster market. Thus was born the Porsche 928, which—to the delight of fans—was built using nothing but Porsche parts.

›› Down in front!

With the front-engine placement of the 928, Porsche seemed determined to leave behind its history of the air-cooled rear engine. The water-cooled V8 front engine was a pioneering design, and sparked a lot of interest in the model even before it was shown to the public.

Built to impress

Customers were thrilled by the changes to the 928. These included comfortable seating for four and an adjustable steering wheel, which also allowed for repositioning of the instrument cluster. The car also had power windows, a central locking system, and headlights that could be retracted when not in use. Most appealing to drivers was the extremely powerful engine. The 928S version, with a top speed of 155 mph (249 km/h), joined the ranks of the world's fastest **production cars**.

When it was launched in 1978, the 928 became the very first sports car to win the title Car of the Year.

Porsche introduced several versions of the 924, including the popular Porsche 944 Turbo. The Turbo marked Porsche's first release of a turbocharged production car in almost ten years.

Risky Business

In the 1983 movie, "Risky Business," a young Tom Cruise plays a teenager left at home alone by his parents—and alone with his father's Porsche 928S. Porsche lovers must have been horrified when the sports car ended up at the bottom of Lake Michigan!

New engine

The biggest improvement was the four-cylinder V8 water-cooled engine, with a top speed of 130 mph (209 km/h). The body was similar to that of the 924 but with changes that included the addition of spoilers, driving lights, and air dams.

Getting it right

The Porsche 944 was a great improvement on the 924, which had left many American drivers less than impressed. Introduced to the United States in 1981, the 944 added a much-appreciated boost to the company's overall sales in America. Many considered the 944 the best sports car in its price range, at US$27,000.

Vital Statistics

944 Turbo Coupe

Production years: 1985–88
No. built: 17,627
Top speed: 152 mph (245 km/h)
Engine type: Inline V8, water-cooled, front-placement
Engine size: 2479 cc (2.5 liter), 217 bhp
Cylinders: 4
Transmission: 5-speed manual
CO_2 emissions: Unknown
EPA fuel economy ratings: 23 mpg (city); 33.2 mpg (highway)
Price: US$33,285 (1988)

Four on the floor

Then came the 964 series. In a nod to tradition, Porsche returned the engine to the rear of the car but surprised everyone by changing the drivetrain to four-wheel drive! The control offered by the Carrera 4 helped draw attention away from Porsche's competitors at the time. It also met the requirement of appealing to a broader buying public.

How cool is that!

The Carrera 4 had a 250 hp engine, with a top speed of 162 mph (260 km/h). It could go from 0 to 60 mph (97 km/h) in under six seconds. One very striking feature of the Carrera 4 was its rear spoiler, which retracted into the rear of the car when it traveled under 49 mph (80 km/h).

Crowd appeal

Some drivers still wanted the option of rear-wheel drive, so later that year Porsche released the Carrera 2. Other versions included the 964 Targa, Carrera 2 Cabriolet, and the Carrera 4 Restyling. The 964 Carrera 2 Cabriolet in 1990 came with two- and four-wheel drive and an attractive fabric roof. It would be one of Porsche's best sellers until series production ended in 1993.

A new look for the 911

The Porsche 993 set out to do what many in the auto industry thought was impossible: improve on the 911. The new 911 (Type 993) was an evolution of the classic design. Most of the changes were inside the car and under the hood. Porsche had promised 30 percent new technology and almost 85 percent new parts. The 993 had greatly improved **traction**, thanks to the new multilink suspension and **transverse** arms.

The 993 Targa

The Targa version of the 993 was very popular among Porsche enthusiasts. It was the first to have the Varioram engine system. The Varioram provided higher or lower air intake, helping the six-cylinder engine reach 14 hp more than the other 993 cars, and allowed for a top speed of 171 mph (275 km/h).

■ The 993 had softer edges and
■ a wider rear end, and the boxer
▼ engine increased its horsepower
to 272 at 6100 rpm.

❯❯ New directions

In the 1990s, a new company president brought more changes to Porsche. As part of an initiative to improve sales opportunities for the company, Porsche set out to increase its car-production roster with some exciting additions. Enter the Porsche 996—a completely new look for the 911 in 1997.

The 996

The 996 had little in common with the existing 911. In fact, it was more like the Boxster, with its powerful rear engine. The boxer engine of the 996 could reach 300 hp at 6800 rpm, allowing an **acceleration** of 0 to 60 mph (97 km/h) in 5.2 seconds. Outside changes included a larger windshield, which helped improve visibility for the driver.

The 996 saw an increase in the use of strong molded plastic in place of metal. This greatly reduced the cost of the car for consumers, as well as making the 996 lighter than previous models. Later versions included the 996 Carrera 4, with four-wheel drive, and an open-top 996 Cabriolet—which was greeted excitedly by fans.

The latest 911

The Porsche 997 is Porsche's most recent version of the 911. The 997 marked the company's return to offering two different engines to customers, the basic and the "S" (for "super"). The basic engine offers 325 hp at 6800 rpm, and the more powerful of the pair, the S engine, produces 355 hp at 6600 rpm.

New Carreras

Production of the new 911 began in 2005 with the 997 Carrera and Carrera S coupes. Changes for the 997 include a new side-door airbag as well as the popular fabric roof that can be fully retracted within 20 seconds. In 2009, the 997 was one of the first Porsche cars to receive the updated Porsche *Doppelkupplung* (PDK) seven-speed **dual-clutch** transmission, which allowed for smooth automatic and manual shifting with no interruption in power.

In 2001, all engines in the 996 models were upgraded to increase the top speed to 177 mph (285 km/h).

Some of the 997 series, including the Carrera 4, offer the popular glass canopy design.

The PSM system

The 996 featured the brand new Porsche Safety Management (PSM) system. A standard feature on all 996s, the PSM system allowed the driver to direct the power of each wheel on the car. This allowed for a better, safer system of traction control.

Chapter 5

On and Off the Track

Everyone knows about Porsche on the roads and racetracks, but there was another popular place for Porsche—the farm! Even before the creation of the famous 356, Ferdinand Porsche Sr. had been working on making a better tractor. Using many of the designs that would appear in his road vehicles, he helped revolutionize the world of farm machinery.

Early work

As far back as the early 1930s, Ferdinand Sr. had designed several prototypes for tractor engines. His first efforts were gasoline-powered only, as he was still working on the finishing touches for a diesel engine—the standard fuel for farm machinery. He eventually perfected his diesel tractor engine, and much like the 356 that would follow, it was air-cooled as well.

Interrupted ... again

As well as working on a "people's car," the Volkswagen, Porsche had been busy designing a people's tractor. This would be a powerful, reliable machine that was affordable by most farmers. But Germany's efforts in World War II forced Ferdinand Sr. to abandon the project to focus on military vehicles. He turned the design project over to his son, Ferry.

The Porsche tractor

By the early 1950s, Porsche had four working designs for a diesel engine tractor. But after the war, only German companies that had been making tractors before the war were allowed to manufacture them. Porsche was a design-firm only, so it had to team up with an already established tractor maker.

The Porsche Junior model, discontinued in 1960, had an air-cooled, 822 cc, single-cylinder, 14 hp engine.

Allgaier partnership

Porsche joined forces with Allgaier and set about making Porsche diesel engine tractors with an Allgaier body. The partnership would continue until about 1956, when Allgaier was bought out by Mannesmann AG. Over the next seven years, almost 125,000 Porsche diesel tractors were made, many of which would find their way to the United States.

Tractor power

All Porsche diesel tractor engines featured Porsche's hydraulic coupling between the engine and transmission. Some of the more popular models included the Porsche 122 Diesel, the Porsche Junior, and the Porsche Super. The considerably more powerful Super model's engine was also air-cooled, with a four-stroke, 2625 cc, three-cylinder engine. The Porsche Diesel Master could get up to almost 20 mph (32 km/h), which is pretty fast for a tractor! Most Porsche tractors are popular today among collectors.

►► A winning record

The Porsche name has always been synonymous with racing. Leaving behind the souped-up 356s and early Spyders of the 1950s and 1960s, Porsche went on to create the engines and cars that would lead the pack on tracks around the world. Success in the 1970s included victories in the CanAm Series, the 24 Hours of Daytona, the 24 Hours of Le Mans, and the World Constructors' Championship.

Kurzcheck and Carrera

For the 1970 season, the rules were changed to include up to five-liter capacity cars at Le Mans. Porsche responded with the Kurzcheck Coupe of the 917 series, with its powerful 12-cylinder engine.

The 911 Carrera RS was a big hit during the 1973 racing season, bringing home wins at three international and seven national championships. The RSR dominated at the GT European Championship that year as well, winning in all its races.

935 and 936

The 1976 Porsche 935 Coupe was known for its distinctive horizontal adjustable **airfoil**. It was powered by an air-cooled six-cylinder turbo engine, with a top speed of 211 mph (340 km/h). The following year, the 936 Spyder—built specifically for the 1977 FIA World Sports Car Championship—demonstrated more racing finesse. It had a large air inlet opening above the driver's seat, as well as a high tail fin. The Spyder had a top speed of almost 205 mph (330 km/h).

935/78 Coupe

The colorful 935/78 racer earned the nickname "Moby Dick" because of its whalelike appearance. Fun to look at, the car dominated the endurance races at the FIA World Sports Car Championship. Its six-cylinder, 750 hp engine could make a top speed of 227 mph (356 km/h).

The first Porsche won a race less than one week after it was finished. Since then, Porsche racecars have been winning races at major motor sports events all over the world.

The FIA

The Federation Internationale de l'Automobile is responsible for enforcing the rules and regulations for motor sports around the world. Formed in 1904, the FIA has its main offices in Paris, France. It governs over 226 motor-sport organizations.

The 1977 Porsche 936/77 Spyder won Porsche its first victory for a turbocharged car at Le Mans.

Vital Statistics

Porsche 935/78 Coupe

Production years: 1978
No. built: 1
Top speed: 227 mph (356 km/h)
Engine type: Water/air-cooled,
Engine size: 3211 cc (3.2 liter),
   750 bhp
Cylinders: 6
Transmission: 4-speed manual
CO_2 emissions: N/A
EPA fuel economy ratings: N/A
Price: N/A

▶▶ In the 1980s

In 1984, the FIA announced that there would be a fuel reduction for Group C cars. This meant Porsche would have to find a way for its C car to use less fuel but still be able to perform. The answer came in the new Motronic electronic fuel-injection system.

The new system proved to be a big success. Placed in the Porsche 962 C, it helped Porsche win the 1,000 km of Mugello race in 1985. That same year, the Porsche 956 C took the 24 hour race at Le Mans, finishing the grueling endurance test with almost 140 liters of fuel still in its tank!

Vital Statistics

Porsche 962

Production years: 1984
No. built: 1
Top speed: 217.5 mph (350 km/h)
Engine type: Air-cooled
Engine size: 2869 cc (2.9 liter), 680 bhp
Cylinders: 6
Transmission: 5-speed manual
CO_2 emissions: N/A
EPA fuel economy ratings: N/A
Price: N/A

This is the Porsche 956 that raced in the 1983 24 Hours of Le Mans.

936/81 Spyder

The 936/81 Spyder blew away the competition at Le Mans in 1981, on the thirtieth anniversary of Porsche's first entry in the race. Its engine produced 620 hp at 8000 rpm, reaching a top speed of almost 224 mph (360 km/h).

Armed with the new Motronic fuel-injection system, the 956 C Coupe earned a win at the 1983 World Endurance Championship, as well as a victory at the Group C Drivers' Championship in Japan. The 956 C had a top speed of over 217.5 mph (350 km/h).

Porsche 962

Made as a 1984-season replacement for the 956, the 962 had a six-cylinder air-cooled engine with a five-speed transmission and a top speed of almost 217.5 mph (350 km/h). This impressive racer would go on to earn victories at the World Endurance Championship, Le Mans, and IMSA racing.

The Porsche 962, produced in 1984, became arguably the most successful sports car in history.

AMAZING FACTS

Porsche 944 Turbo Cup

This four-cylinder speedster would become the overall season leader in 1986. Its water-cooled engine could reach speeds of almost 152 mph (245 km/h).

The IMSA

The International Motor Sports Association (IMSA) is an organization for motor-sport events in the United States. Founded in the early 1970s, it oversees competitions such as the American Le Mans, GT3 Cup, and Formula BMW USA.

» The 1990s and beyond

Porsche decided to focus much of its efforts on the American CART series in the 1990s. It completely reworked the Porsche-March 89 P Cart, which had finished fourth in the drivers' standing for the 1989 season. Now called the 90P, it had a more compact gearbox, and weight distribution was improved by moving the fuel tank and the turbocharger. Porsche was also able to maintain its winning history in other events, with victories at Le Mans in 1994 and the Rolex 24 at Daytona (formerly 24 Hours at Daytona).

911 GTs

The GT2 had a strong resemblance to its production-car counterpart. It was a regular winner of long-distance competitions and featured a flat six-cylinder engine producing 450 hp at 5750 rpm. It could reach a top speed of 186 mph (300 km/h). The GT3 R earned Porsche another impressive win at Le Mans in 1999. Its Multi-Point Fuel Injection (MPI) system allowed for a better distribution of mixture into each of the engine cylinders. The GT3 R had a top speed of almost 190 mph (306 km/h).

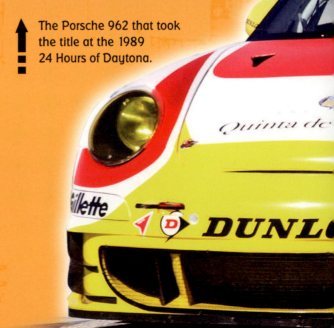

The Porsche 962 that took the title at the 1989 24 Hours of Daytona.

Racing today

More than a decade into the new century, the racing works of Porsche have already amassed an impressive list of victories. Armed with the powerful 911 series, Le Mans continues to be the staging ground for new Porsche racing models looking to dominate the competition. A Class victory at Le Mans in 2000 showed the racing community what the new 911 GT3 Cup was capable of. It also won at the FIA GT International Championship.

The Porsche 911 GT3 RSR has won at both Le Mans and the Nürburgring 24-hour races.

Porsche 911 GT3 RSR

The GT3 RSR is the most powerful Porsche racer based on its 911 production design. Its distinctive front section has a large ventilation opening on the hood. The engine delivers 450 hp at 7800 rpm.

RS Spyder

Begun in 2005, the RS Spyder is all Porsche. Its extremely powerful eight-cylinder engine produces 440 hp at 9000 rpm. It has recorded many major wins, including honors at Le Mans in 2008 and 2009.

Chapter 6

>> Today and Tomorrow >>>>>>

The mid-1980s and early 1990s were not a great time for Porsche financially. Car-development programs were proving very costly. Sales of the 924, 928, 944, and 968 had not developed in the way the company had hoped. In fact, sales in the United States had been dropping steadily since 1987—from 30,471 that year to 3,728 in 1993. It looked like the public might be losing interest in Porsche's formerly popular 911 series.

In need of a change

These were dark times for the automaker. There were concerns that Porsche may have left itself open to being taken over by another company. Having turned away from its successful history of rear-placement air-cooled engines, Porsche found itself in a much-needed overhaul. Few outside the company knew, however, that plans were already underway for the small automaker to turn its luck around—and in a big way!

Porsche museum

Completed in 2009, the Porsche museum stands near the company's headquarters in Stuttgart. It features over 80 vehicles on display. Exhibits include both famous and forgotten models alike, as well as the technical achievements of the company.

The Porsche museum is housed in an impressive building in the Zuffenhausen area of Stuttgart, close to the company's headquarters.

In 1992, things got so bad for Porsche that it had to let go of 1,850 factory workers—almost 25 percent of its workforce.

The dynamic duo

Following its new strategy, Porsche was busy getting ready to release its next generation of cars. The company dropped its plans for a four-door vehicle and rushed project numbers 996 and 986 into completion. Project 996 was an all-new 911, and project 986 was the more-affordable Boxster.

Cost cutting

To help save money, Porsche decided to develop both cars at the same time, cutting back on costs and helping make the vehicles less expensive when they went on the market. The two models would also share many of the same parts. Hopes were high at Porsche, even though the new 911 would have to meet with the approval of the 911 community of drivers, and the Boxster would be going up against new models produced by competitors such as Mercedes-Benz and BMW.

The next stage for Porsche

The world got its first look at Porsche's Boxster at the 1996 Paris Motor Show. With the company in a slump, everyone was anxious to see what Porsche had in mind for its new model. The Boxster's shape was a look back to the lines and curves of the now-legendary 550 Spyder. It was very pleasing to the eye. People also took notice of Porsche's latest engineering accomplishment. Placed just ahead of the rear axle, this was the first of Porsche's new water-cooled flat-six engines.

The look and power of Porsche's newest two-seater caused quite the commotion! The new engine produced 204 hp at 6000 rpm, with a top speed of 149 mph (240 km/h).

A home run for Porsche

Production of the Boxster began later that year. Even in a market dominated by newer sporting models, the Boxster was a big hit with drivers and members of the auto industry. It was such a success, in fact, that the Porsche factory in Stuttgart was overwhelmed with orders. Porsche was forced to use another factory in Finland to help keep up with the growing demand.

The 911 GT3 RS is one of the latest—and fastest—in the new 911 series.

Meet the new 911

A year after the Boxster debuted, Porsche presented the other half of its next generation of cars. The 911 Carrera resembled its counterpart in its front end, and the interior was a completely new approach to the series. The new 911 began to make waves as soon as it was revealed at the 1997 Frankfurt Auto Show.

While the new 911 shared many parts with the Boxster, it had more than enough features to set it apart. The engine was the first use of a water-cooled six-cylinder boxer engine inside a production 911 car. The flashy rear spoiler rolled out automatically when the car reached speeds of 75 mph (121 km/h). Like the Boxster, the 911 was a hit, helping to rejuvenate interest in the 911 series.

Vital Statistics

986 Boxster

Production years: 1997–99
No. built: 55,705
Top speed: 149 mph (240 km/h)
Engine type: Air-cooled, mid-engine
Engine size: 2480 cc (2.5 liter), 204 bhp
Cylinders: 6
Transmission: 5-speed manual; 5-speed Tiptronic optional
CO_2 emissions: 239 g/km
EPA fuel economy ratings: 19.7 mpg (city); 39.7 mpg (highway)
Price: 79,210 Deutschmarks (approx. US$ 41,000) (1998)

The Cayenne

Porsche has never been known to rest on past success—or shy away from a challenge. With the announcement of the Cayenne S, Porsche officially set its sights on conquering a previously unexplored area—the sport-utility vehicle (SUV) market. It was a bold move for the company, but one that would prove successful.

The Cayenne front-engine SUV went into production in 2002. Initially two versions were offered, the Cayenne S and Cayenne Turbo. Both versions of the Cayenne were fully off-road capable, had four large doors for passengers and driver, and seated five comfortably.

Cayenne power

The Cayenne model came with a water-cooled V8 engine with six-speed transmission for both versions. The Cayenne S had a top speed of 150 mph (241 km/h), and the Turbo a top speed of 165 mph (251 km/h). With the release of a "basic" version of the car in 2004, drivers also had the option of a six-cylinder, 250 hp, 6000 rpm engine.

The Cayenne Turbo S can go from 0 to 60 mph (97 km/h) in 4.9 seconds.

Vital Statistics

Cayenne Turbo S

Production years: 2003–
No. built: Still in production
Top speed: 165 mph (255 km/h)
Engine type: Water-cooled, front-placement
Engine size: 4511 cc, 9.5 liter, 450 hp
Cylinders: 8
Transmission: 6-speed manual
CO_2 emissions: 378 g/km
EPA fuel economy ratings: 12.9 mpg (city); 23.7 mpg (highway)
Price: US$130,443 (100,024 euros)

Come sail away

The latest addition to the Cayenne family is the Cayenne S Hybrid. The 333 hp V6 engine works together with a 47 hp electric motor to help improve fuel efficiency in the SUV. The motor can also be used to give the Cayenne S Hybrid a boost when pulling into traffic or passing. There is also the new "sailing" mode, in which the engine disengages automatically when the driver releases the throttle. The SUV then coasts along until the driver accelerates, automatically reengaging the engine.

The Porsche Communication Management (PCM) system offered a radio, *GPS*, and hands-free telephone access.

AMAZING FACTS

Cayenne changes

Aside from the engine, the basic version differed little from the Cayenne S. The front brake discs were slightly smaller in the basic Cayenne. Inside the basic version, black was used on the instrument bezels and around the gear lever instead of silver.

Tiptronic S

Tiptronic S is a combination of automatic and manual transmission. When in automatic, the system allows for multiple shifting points for each gear. This makes for higher-performance driving and lower fuel consumption.

⟩⟩ The Cayman

Porsche recognized there was a gap between the Boxster and the more powerful 911 series. Drivers wanted the next step up from the Boxster— but without the considerable increase in price of the 911. The Cayman S provided drivers with the next level in speed and power while taking it easy on their wallets. Initially, the idea was to give the existing Boxster a tune-up, increasing power and speed, then swapping out its body for a coupe design. In the end, though, Porsche decided to go with a more distinctive two-door, mid-engine coupe.

What's in a name?

The cayman, or caiman, is a reptile found in South America. Closely related to the alligator, the cayman's belly is protected by a layer of bony plates. Some caymans can grow up to 20 feet (six m) in length and are known for being able to move very quickly over short distances on land. The cayman is also very agile in water and is prone to attack.

↑ Plans for the mid-engine Cayman S had been several years in the making.

 Launched in 2006, the Cayman S featured a 320 hp, 7200 rpm engine and had a top speed of 172 mph (277 km/h). The price was midway between the Boxster and 911 cars.

Cayman power

The Cayman S came in rear-wheel drive and six-speeds, with either a manual or Porsche *Doppelkupplung* (PDK) dual-clutch transmission. Little changed in terms of appearance with the release of the basic version, the Cayman, a year later. There was a slight difference with the Cayman's rear suspension. The engine could do 0 to 60 mph (97 km/h) in just over six seconds, and the car had a top speed of 165 mph (266 km/h). In 2010, the Automotive Performance Execution and Layout Study (APEAL) voted the Cayman the "Ideal Sports Car."

Vital Statistics

Cayman S

Production years: 2006–
No. built: Still in production
Top speed: 172 mph (277 km/h)
Engine type: Water-cooled, mid-placement
Engine size: 3.4 liter, 320 hp
Cylinders: 6
Transmission: 5-speed manual Tiptronic (optional PDK)
CO_2 emissions: 230 g/km
EPA fuel economy ratings: 19 mpg (city); 26 mpg (highway)
Price: US$61,500

>> The Panamera

In 2009, Porsche surprised the auto industry again with another leap forward—the Panamera. Named after the world-famous endurance race, the Carrera Panamerica, Porsche's latest creation combined the comfort and space of a **sedan** with the power and speed of a sports car. The final result debuted in China at Auto Shanghai 2009.

Initial reaction to the Panamera was mixed. Some questioned the car's appearance, with its rather bulbous rear end. Others praised the powerful front engine and amount of seating and storage space. Production began that year at Porsche's state-of-the-art plant in Leipzig, Germany.

The first release

The Panamera S, 4S, and Turbo versions were first off the line in Leipzig. Both the S and 4S versions featured 400 hp engines, and the Porsche Active Suspension Management (PASM) system. It was equipped with a high-tech center console. The heated seats and color touchscreen audio system helped to emphasize the level of comfort Porsche was advertising.

Turbocharged

The Panamera Turbo had an impressive top speed of 188 mph (303 km/h), thanks to its 500 hp, 6000 rpm engine. The all-wheel-drive, eight-cylinder engine provided the additional speed and power expected of a turbo Porsche.

As with the rest of the Panamera series, the engine of the Turbo was placed in the front of the car. The Porsche Turbo was the most expensive of the series, costing almost US$135,300.

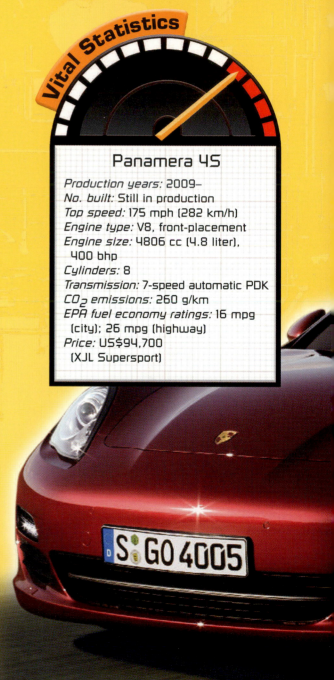

Vital Statistics

Panamera 4S

Production years: 2009–
No. built: Still in production
Top speed: 175 mph (282 km/h)
Engine type: V8, front-placement
Engine size: 4806 cc (4.8 liter), 400 bhp
Cylinders: 8
Transmission: 7-speed automatic PDK
CO_2 emissions: 260 g/km
EPA fuel economy ratings: 16 mpg (city); 26 mpg (highway)
Price: US$94,700 (XJL Supersport)

The all-wheel drive of the Panamera 4S allowed for a slightly faster acceleration over the rear-wheel drive of the Panamera S.

The Panamera signaled Porsche's return to the four-door sedan. Porsche designers were uncompromising in their determination to blend performance and comfort in the new model.

PASM

Porsche Active Suspension Management (PASM) allows for the adjustment of the car's suspension. One setting offers a more relaxed and comfortable suspension. The other firms up the suspension considerably, allowing for the agile and sporty feel associated with a sports car.

The future of Porsche

Porsche recovered from its financial worries of the early 1990s and today is focusing on maintaining the success of its next generation of cars. The Porsche market is growing in countries beyond the United States and Germany. China has recently become Porsche's biggest market for the Cayenne series.

In 2009, Porsche failed in a bid to take over the much larger automaker Volkswagen. Since then, Volkswagen has been working with Porsche on a merger of the two companies. With plans to make Porsche its tenth brand, Volkswagen acquired nearly half of Porsche's shares by 2010, with plans to acquire the rest in 2011. Volkswagen also assumed control of Porsche's German car manufacturing in 2010 as part of the merger.

Era of the hybrid

Porsche is hoping to lead the market in hybrid sports cars. It revealed its work on the 918 Spyder at the Geneva Auto Show in 2010. This mid-engine sports car features plug-in hybrid technology, with twin electric motors that work with the V8 engine for a combined 718 hp. The 918 Spyder is able to run in "electric mode" much longer than other hybrids, with a top speed of 198 mph (319 km/h). Thanks to the overwhelming response from the public, Porsche has moved from **concept car** to pre-production vehicle, with trials set to begin in 2011.

As a "plug-in" hybrid, the 918 Spyder's batteries can be charged from a power outlet—just like a cell phone or mp3 player!

 Porche's new 911 GT3 R Hybrid
has performed wonderfully at
the Le Mans and Nürburgring
24-hour competitions.

Green racing

Porsche is also working to take its hybrid
initiative to the racetrack, with the 911
GT3 R Hybrid. This machine has two
electric motors on the front axle and a
480 hp rear engine. Instead of using a
battery, as other hybrids do, the 911 GT3 R
Hybrid converts the kinetic energy from
braking into electricity. When the car
accelerates, the gathered electricity is
used to power the front wheels. This
helps the racecar conserve fuel, and it
can be used as a boost when overtaking
other cars on the track.

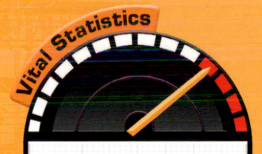

Vital Statistics

911 GT3 R Hybrid

Production years: Still in
   development
No. built: 1 (prototype)
Top speed: Unknown
Engine type: Flat-six (60 kw motors
   in front)
Engine size: 4-liter, 480 bhp
Cylinders: 6
Transmission: 6-speed manual
CO_2 emissions: N/A
EPA fuel economy ratings: N/A
Price: N/A

Porsche Timeline

1931	Ferdinand Porsche Sr. founds the Porsche company
1939	Porsche designs the Type 60K10
1944	Porsche moves operations from Germany to Austria
1948	Prototype 356/1 is revealed
1949	356/2 is shown at the Geneva Auto Show
1951	Ferdinand Porsche Sr. dies
1952	Production of the 356 American Roadster
1954	550 Spyder is put into production
1955	Launch of the Porsche Speedster
1956	356A is launched; Porsche wins its first Targa Florio
1960	356B is launched
1962	Porsche wins its first Grand Prix, in France
1963	Porsche 911 is unveiled at the Frankfurt Motor Show
1965	Production starts on the 911 Coupe
1967	911 Targa is released
1969	Porsche collaborates with Volkswagen on the 914
1973	911 Carrera RS is a big hit in the racing season
1975	Porsche releases the 924 to replace the 914
1977	Turbo version of the 924 is produced; 936/77 gets Porsche its first win at Le Mans
1978	The 928 wins Car of the Year in the year of its release
1981	The 944 is introduced in America; Porsche wins at Le Mans
1984	The 924 is reintroduced as the 924S
1985	Production begins on the 944 Turbo Coupe; Porsche wins the 1,000 km of Mugello race
1992	Porsche faces financial difficulties and makes cuts at its factories
1994	The 911 is revamped as the Type 993
1996	Porsche Boxster is unveiled at the Paris Motor Show
1997	The 996 is released as the new-look 911; 986 Boxster goes into production
2002	Cayenne SUV goes into production
2006	Work begins on the Cayenne S
2008	RS Spyder wins at Le Mans
2009	Panamera is launched; all-new Porsche Museum is completed
2010	Hybrid 918 Spyder is shown at the Geneva Auto Show

Further Information

Books

Porsche Data Book
by Marc Bongers
(Haynes Publishing, 2009)

Porsche: The Ultimate Guide
by Scott Farger
(KP Books, 2005)

Porsche
by Lisa Bullard
(Capstone Press, 2008)

Hot Cars: Porsche
by Lee Stacy
(Rourke Publishing, 2005)

Web sites

www.porsche.com
The official web site of the Porsche company

www.porsche.com/international/aboutporsche/
porschemuseum/
The area of the Porsche web site dedicated to the Porsche
museum in Stuttgart

www.gtpurelyporsche.com/
The web site of the magazine GT Porsche

Glossary

acceleration A measure of how quickly something speeds up

airfoil A device used on a vehicle to control stability and help propulsion

concept car A vehicle made to show the public a new design or technology

coupe A hard-topped sports car with two seats

dual clutch A form of transmission system that allows for shifting between manual and automatic

flagship The model that best represents a brand

GPS (global positioning system) A satellite-based system that can identify the position of a car and give directions to a destination

horsepower (hp) The amount of pulling power an engine has, calculated as the number of horses it would take to pull the same load

hybrid car A car that uses both a regular combustion engine and an electric system

hydraulic Something that is powered or operated by water

imported Brought into a country from another country to sell

production car A car that is made in large numbers on an assembly line and which will be sold to the public

prototype The original or test version of a car, which is later modified and developed into a production car

roadster A two-seat car that has no roof or side windows

sedan A passenger car with four doors and a back seat

souped-up Modified so as to provide better performance, more speed, or greater efficiency

speedster A car that is especially designed to travel at high speeds

state-of-the-art Referring to the highest level of development at a given time

stock car A standard car that has been altered so it can compete in races

traction The quality of the contact a car has with the road or other surface on which it travels

transmission The device in a car that allows the driver to change gears

transverse Lying across or crossways

turbocharged Of an engine, fitted with a gas compressor to make the vehicle it powers go faster

>> Index

Entries in **bold** indicate pictures